1

I am often asked whether any booI thought I would produce a booklet based on f collecting and growing them. In a bookl begin the complicated question of botanica Therefore I have loosely grouped together the .... out by type and geographical location. Although this may not be botanically correct, I think it is better than listing the plants in alphabetical order and I hope it gives some idea of the different types that you are likely to come across including some that have only recently been introduced into the UK by ourselves. Further, more detailed information covering many more species and including classification into subgenera and sections and more detailed botanical descriptions will be included in a book that I am writing which I hope to have published at a later date.

Contents

	Page
Introduction	1
Salvias as Garden Plants	2
Our Collection	2
Sage as a Medicinal Herb	3
Characteristics	4 - 5
Growing conditions	6
Propagation	7
Pollination	8
Pests & Diseases	8
Salvias from the Old World	9 - 30
Salvias from the New World	31 - 52
List of Species	inside back cover

Notes on Plant Descriptions

The name following the species is the name of the botanist who first introduced the plant and the date following is the date of introduction.

Measurements are imperial followed by metric and where two measurements are given together, they are height followed by spread.

Spread is after one seasons growth and may be considerably more with hardy types after several years. Height includes flowers spikes unless otherwise stated.

The only synonyms given are those that you are likely to come across commercially.

Salvias as Garden Plants

Salvia *Linn.* is a genus of 900 species in the Labiatae family. They are closely related to other scented herbs such as rosemary, lavender, mint, marjoram, and savoury. Over 500 species of Salvia are found in the Americas, with the rest being spread all over the temperate and sub - tropical areas of the world except Australasia.

They are highly ornamental flowering plants and they have recently started to become popular as garden plants. Salvia officinalis, the common sage, was at one time one of the most important medicinal herbs. Nowadays it is most commonly used as a seasoning in cooking.

It was not many years ago, that apart from Salvia officinalis, the only Salvia well known in cultivation was Salvia splendens, commonly used as a half hardy summer bedding plant. The genus is however, very diverse, from dwarf shrubs suitable for the rock garden to large herbaceous perennials and woody shrubs.

The hardy species commence flowering in May and if pruned after flowering, many will have repeat flowering throughout the summer. The half hardy and tender species commence flowering from July onwards and continue until November or even later if the weather is mild. Many species from the more tropical areas will not begin flowering until late summer or autumn and some will rarely flower outdoors in this country unless in exceptionally mild areas, usually by the coast, and these are best treated as winter flowering conservatory plants.

Our Collection

We have been collecting and growing Salvias since 1978 when very few were available. There are now around 200 species available in this country, many of which are only obtainable from very few nurseries and some at the moment still only from ourselves.

There are three NCCPG National Collections of Salvia of which ours is one. Our collection of around 200 species was designated as a National Collection in 1992 and is planted in a special area of our garden which is open to the public on special Salvia days and to groups by prior appointment.

Although we are situated in South Devon, we are very exposed and many of the plants are not hardy with us and have to be replaced each year.
We propagate the plants for sale in our nursery and by mail order and although we cannot have all the varieties available for sale at one time, we hope to always have a good selection available.

Sage as a Medicinal Herb

Fresh leaves of Salvia officinalis, the common sage are used to make a drink which is said to cool a fever and purify the blood. A strong infusion of the leaves without the lemon and sugar is used as a lotion to heal ulcers and raw abrasions of the skin.

Sage tea was said to help with many ailments such as nervous disorders, delirium of fever, weak digestion, typhoid, sickness, liver and kidney problems, nervous headache, haemorrhage from lungs or stomach, colds in the head, sore throats, quinsy and palsy as well as to stop excessive perspiration.

It was at one time, a common ingredient in tooth powders and it is said that fresh leaves rubbed on the teeth will clean them and strengthen the gums.
Dried leaves smoked in a pipe are said to be good as a remedy for asthma.
The juice of sage in warm water with vinegar was at one time used as a cure for the plague.
The volatile oil is a violent epileptiform convulsant resembling the oils of absinthe and nutmeg and when inhaled for some time it causes giddiness.

The oil from Salvia sclarea is known commercially as Clary Oil or Muscatel Sage and is mainly used as a fixer in the perfume industry. An infusion of the leaves of S. sclarea is used for stomach and kidney disorders. In Jamaica a mixture of the leaves boiled in coconut oil was used to cure scorpion stings.
A wine is made by boiling the leaves and flowers of S. sclarea with sugar.

An infusion of the leaves of Salvia viridis is used as a gargle for sore throats and the powdered, dried leaves make a good snuff.

At one time a distilled water of the leaves of Salvia verbenaca was used as an eye wash.

In Holland, the leaves of Salvia glutinosa are used to give flavour to country wines.

In Greece and the Greek islands, Salvia pomifera produces galls as a defence against an insect. These galls are known as sage apples and they are candied with sugar and made into a sweetmeat and conserve which is regarded by the Greeks as a great delicacy. The leaves are collected annually and before sunrise on the 1st of May is regarded as the best time to do this. The leaves are also dried and made into an infusion which induces perspiration.

Characteristics

Aromatic foliage
Opposite leaves
Square stems
Calyx with three upper and two lower spines
Flowers have two lips (bilabiate) giving the family name Labiatae
Two stamens only

All have aromatic foliage, some more noticeable than others. The aromatic oils are produced by the epidermal glands and these help to prevent the foliage being eaten by animals and help to prevent desiccation by the strong sun. Some species with particularly strong aromatic foliage are, S. elegans, pomifera. tingitana, africana - lutea and clevelandii. In some species the whole plant is aromatic e.g. S. mellifera, keerlii and sclarea which is particularly pungent with the aroma of ambergris but more commonly compared to that of sweaty socks.

All have opposite leaves which can be of three types -
a) Basal leaves, either forming a rosette e.g. S. pratensis and S. staminea or a large basal clump e.g. S. forskaohlei and S. castanea.
b) Stem leaves. These are not always present when basal leaves are present e.g. S. argentea. When in conjunction with basal leaves they are usually smaller and often different e.g. S. barrelieri, either with a shorter leaf stalk (petiolate) or without (sessile). In the case of a shrub or bushy perennial species, the leaves are all stem leaves and distributed all over the plant. e.g. S. microphylla.
c) Flower stem leaves. These can be the same as the stem leaves or adapted to form bracts which are often coloured and may fall as the buds open (deciduous) e.g. S. fulgens or remain when the flowers open (persistent), in which case they are often as colourful and attractive as the flowers e.g. S. sclarea.

The leaves are usually simple (only one leaflet) or can be pinnate (with several pairs of leaflets arranged on either side of a central stalk) e.g. S. interrupta.
The leaf margins can be smooth (entire) e.g. S. greggii; fringed with hairs (ciliate) e.g. S. blepharophylla or be variously lobed, e.g. S. argentea; serrate e.g. S. uliginosa; crenate e.g. S. leucophylla or pinnatisect e.g. S. caespitosa. Margins may also be undulate e.g. S. dominica. The surface of the leaves is sometimes without hairs (glabrous) e.g. S. miniata but more often covered in some kind of indumentum e.g. S. amarissima with both surfaces hairy or S. campanulata with beige tomentum beneath. The surface may also be rough and wrinkled (rugose) e.g. S. pomifera and the colour of the leaves apart from various shades of green, may be grey e.g. S. lanceolata; almost white e.g. S. apiana or purple e.g. S. sinaloensis.

All have square stems, some particularly noticeable, such as S. madrensis which has thick, stout, deeply ribbed stems up to one inch square. Stems are usually hairy in varying degrees and are often also woody towards the base of the plant.

The flowers are arranged in false whorls (verticillasters) on either a spike, e.g. S. nemorosa; a raceme, e.g. S. iodantha; or a panicle. e.g. S. candelabrum.
A whorl can consist of only one pair of flowers e.g. S. microphylla or can have a large number of flowers crowding together to form a dense, globular head (glomerule) e.g. S. mellifera, or any amount between the two extremes. The whorls are sometimes well spaced on the stem e.g. S. patens or close together so as to be almost continuous e.g. S. confertiflora.

The corolla is formed by the petals joining together to form a tube with two lips. The tube may be only partially protruding from the calyx (included) e.g. S. virgata or fully protruding (exserted) e.g. S. elegans, and may also be inflated. e.g. S. involucrata. There are always two stamens. These may occasionally be exserted from the corolla. e.g. S. austriaca. The upper lip may be hooded e.g. S. patens or straight e.g. S. scabra. The bottom lip consists of three lobes. The tube and particularly the upper lip may be covered in hairs, occasionally giving a velvety appearance e.g. S. blepharophylla. There are often markings, usually white, in the throat of the corolla e.g. S. africana - caerulea.

The calyx is formed by the sepals joining together and it has two lips, the upper usually having three spines and the lower only two. It may be green e.g. S. cacaliaefolia or a completely different colour e.g. S. van houttii. It may fall with the corolla e.g. S. concolor, or may persist after the corolla has fallen e.g. S. verticillata and may enlarge with the formation of the seed e.g. S. pomifera. The size of the calyx varies considerably and is not dependent on the size of the flower. It may be without hairs (glabrous) e.g. S. atrocyanea or glandular hairy e.g. S. glutinosa so that it sticks to the fur of passing animals to be carried to another area, or be covered in long, coloured hairs e.g. S. leucantha.

There are three types of roots. As well as ordinary fibrous roots some species have underground runners e.g. S. blepharophylla and S. uliginosa with which the plant spreads. Other species have tuberous roots e.g. S. patens and S. guaranitica. These can be dried and stored over winter in the same way as dahlia tubers.

Growing Conditions

Salvias do best in our climate in a light, well drained soil with a little lime and in a sunny position. Too much nitrogen with some species will result in a lot of growth but few flowers, therefore summer feeding should consist of a high potash feed. Those plants kept in pots will require more feeding than those grown in the ground. Many of the species that are fairly frost hardy may succumb to our wet weather. Very few of the Salvias like moist conditions and most will not tolerate wet with frost. Therefore all Salvias, even those that come from wet areas in their native country are best grown in a free draining soil in this country e.g. S. uliginosa grows in wet ground as its name implies. It may perform very slightly better in moister ground but this will reduce its chances of surviving the winter in the open. We have always grown it in the same area as our other Salvias and found that it always survives as low as -6°C unprotected and will probably take quite a bit more frost with a protective mulch.

Similarly in their native habitat, many of the Salvias particularly those from more tropical parts grow in shade in the forests. In this country most will grow in full sun, although a few do slightly better with a little shade, particularly those with smooth leaves e.g. S. guaranitica, van houttii and miniata. Also these more tropical types require more humus in the soil, as these will be the ones that require watering first in periods of hot, dry weather.

I am always being asked whether a particular variety will survive outside in the winter or whether I take it in. Most of the Salvias get too large to dig up and put in a pot to over winter with protection. It is preferable to take cuttings in the late summer/autumn and over winter them as young plants in a frost free glasshouse. For those species that set seed, it is advisable to save this as well, as an extra precaution.

Many Salvias become dormant in the winter, i.e. they die down below the ground and hopefully reappear with warmer weather in the spring. Some species such as S. fruticosa survive above the ground and except for extreme conditions will survive the winter unscathed. Others such as S. microphylla are woody shrubs and will often flower throughout the winter given a sheltered spot backed by a wall. In temperatures below -5°C there will be some damage to these types and then they are best pruned in the spring.

The tender perennials are best treated as annuals, being planted out in early summer, with cuttings being taken late summer to over winter under glass ready for the following years plants.

Many of the species from South West USA may not flower if grown as annuals. It is best to over winter an established plant for flowering in the conservatory in early summer. They are spring/early summer flowering in their native habitat and go dormant in their dry summers.

Propagation

Most Salvias, particularly the bushy perennial and shrubby types are easily propagated from cuttings. Those that are particularly hairy or have grey foliage are usually more difficult. Bottom heat and hormone rooting powder are beneficial but not essential for most types. Spring and late summer are the usual times for taking cuttings although they can be taken at any time during the growing season. We find that a mixture of 2/3rd cocoa fibre or peat with 1/3rd sharp sand or vermiculite are equally as good. If the cuttings are very soft it often helps to remove the growing tip and remove most of the leaves or cut larger leaves in half. A 3½" pot is ideal for up to five cuttings. If you do not have a propagation unit, cover the pot with a polythene bag and fasten with an elastic band. When the cuttings have rooted, pot them up into individual small pots, using a ready mixed potting compost such as Levington or similar and transfer to a shady part of the greenhouse. The growing tips should be pinched out regularly to encourage bushy plants. They should be potted up to larger pots when ready and hardened off before planting out in April for hardy species or late May for the tender ones.

Those that do not flower outside in our climate but flower in the winter under glass, are best propagated in mid summer as well if you want to have plants of flowering size for the conservatory in winter, without them being too large.

Many Salvias are often grown from seed, particularly those that do not have obvious cutting material, such as those with basal leaves with few or no stem leaves. Seed can be sown in the same mixture as for cuttings from mid February onwards. Cover lightly, except for very fine seed which is best left uncovered. With gentle bottom heat, most species germinate within a week, although some will take much longer.

However, to ensure the young plants produced are exactly the same as their parents they should be propagated vegetatively i.e. not by seed; but where cutting material is not available, by division, layers, runners, basal shoots etc. This however, is not commercially viable due to the limited amount of plants that can be produced this way compared to the amount easily produced by seed.

Many of these types do usually come true from seed, however there is always the chance that they will have been cross pollinated with other species, producing hybrids between the parents. Plants raised from seed also gives variations, from whence we get the many named forms of some species such as S. nemorosa. Plants grown from seed of cultivars should not be called by the cultivar name.

In our experience most species do not hybridise readily. The exceptions are the microphylla and greggii types which is discussed later.

Pollination

Those species with large flowers mainly cross pollinate and those with small flowers are mainly self pollinated. To explain why some species always set a lot of seed whilst others never produce seed. Briefly, there are three types of flowers. The relative positions of the anthers and the stigmas in different species is directly related to good natural seed setting. The species with the stamens at a lower level than the stigma or vice versa do not easily set seed naturally. Those with small flowers are usually homostylic (having stamens and styles at the same levels) and seed setting is usually high.

Pollinators are humming birds (not in the UK), which usually prefer the red flowered species and butterflies and bees. In some cases such as S. glutinosa and S. coccinea, ants are often pollinators.

Pests and Diseases

The main pests are white fly which can be a particular nuisance under glass, although it does not seem to cause much harm, unlike the leaf hopper which is attracted by the aromatic foliage and which sucks the juices from the leaves making them discoloured and unsightly. A few species are particularly prone to red spider mite, particularly S. concolor which always seems to have this problem with us even outside in the open. Black fly always seems to find the newly opened flowers of S. madrensis, even when flowering outside in the autumn.
Salvia weevils which eat the seed can be a problem in areas where there are many native species.

A view of the Salvia garden at Pleasant View

Geographically Salvias can be divided into two groups, those from the Old World and those from the New World.

The Old World

This covers Europe, Asia, Asia Minor, the Middle East, the Mediterranean, the Balkans and the continent of Africa.

There are about 400 species in this group with 36 of them being native to Europe, 59 from Africa, 86 from Turkey of which 50% are endemic and 70 from Iran with 40% endemism.

Many of these species are frost hardy, although they will not necessarily over-winter unprotected due to our wet climate. Some of these species have grey foliage and the flower colours are mainly pale; often blue, lilac, pink, yellow and white. In their natural habitat these species usually grow on rocky limestone or volcanic slopes or poor stony or sandy ground which is free draining. In spells of hot dry weather those species with grey foliage will cope best and will not usually require watering. Most of these species set seed and are often grown from seed. Some will not flower in the same year as the seed is sown. However if it is not possible to take cuttings they should be propagated wherever possible by division etc. Many die down below the ground in winter and become dormant.

They can be divided into three groups

Group 1

Those species that have foliage that forms a basal rosette or a basal clump from which the flowering stems arise, with few or no stem leaves, flowering in early summer with repeat flowering if pruned. They are practically always grown commercially from seed.

Two species that are native to the UK. -

Salvia verbenaca *Linn.* 1753
syn. S. clandestina
Vervain or Wild Clary

Native of Europe including the UK, North-West & North Africa, Crimea, Caucasus, Cyprus and Palestine.

This is a hardy species which is only suitable for the wild garden as it self seeds so much as to be a nuisance. It would be forgiven if it was particularly attractive, but the blue or pink flowers are so small and hardly protrude from the calyx. The coarse, deeply and irregularly lobed, dark green leaves form a basal rosette with a deep, woody tap root, from which the branched inflorescence arises to a height of 2½ft.(75cm). The stem leaves are few and smaller than the basal leaves and without petioles (sessile).

It is usually grown from seed and an early spring sowing will produce flowering plants by June. Hardy to -15°C.

Salvia pratensis *Linn.* 1753
Meadow Clary

Found in dryish, limestone meadows in Cornwall, Kent & Oxfordshire in the UK, but widely distributed in the rest of Europe. This is a hardy perennial to 2½ x 2½ft.(75 x 75cm), dormant in winter and suitable for sun and partial shade. The dark green leaves are ovate to lanceolate, irregularly notched and mostly basal, forming a rosette in the first year. The few stem leaves are either sessile (without stems) or have shorter stems. The fairly large flowers are a deep purplish blue with a hooded upper lip in whorls of 4-6. Propagation is usually by seed. Hardy to -15°C.

There are many named forms of this species with either just slight variations or completely different colour flowers.

S. pratensis 'Lapis Lazuli' - has large flowers in two shades of pink.
S. pratensis 'Haematodes' - often classed as S. haematodes, a separate species. The flowers are a particularly lovely shade of pale lavender blue (see photo)

Salvia argentea *Linn.* 1753

Native to Southern Europe, Eastern Mediterranean & North-West Africa.

This is a species that is often classed as a biennial, but in our experience it usually lasts several years and it is therefore best treated as a short lived perennial, which dies down below ground in winter. It is frost hardy to -10°C but does not like to be waterlogged and slugs and snails seem to find it appetising. In the first year it forms an attractive, basal rosette of huge, ovate, irregularly lobed leaves which are covered in long, silky hairs giving it a silvery appearance, hence the name argentea, meaning silvery. In June of the following year, a large, branched, pyramidal inflorescence erupts to 3ft.(90cm) tall with many whorls of 4-10 flowers. The large flowers are white with the hooded upper lip having short, violet hairs on the tip. The stems are best cut to the ground after flowering if seed is not required for propagation and you will often get a later succession of flowers. However, it is a very attractive plant for just the foliage alone.

Salvia aethiopis *Linn.* 1753
African Sage

Native to Central & Southern Europe, Western Asia, the Mediterranean & North Africa.

This species is closely related to and similar to S. argentea. However, the leaves are not quite so attractive or hairy and are more serrated than lobed. The large flowers are white, tinged yellowish in whorls of 4-10 with pale green, violet tinged, persistent, hairy bracts on large, pyramidal inflorescences to 3ft.(90cm) tall. Propagation is by seed or division.

Salvia barralieri *Lam.* 1791
syn. S. bicolor
syn. S. dichroa

Native to North Africa & South-West Spain.
This is a hardy, short lived perennial, often classed as a biennial, with large basal leaves forming a clump to 2ft.(60cm) across and often dying back in winter. The bluish grey, broadly ovate leaves are coarsely and irregularly lobed. The stout stems arise to 4ft.(120cm) and are usually unbranched with few stem leaves. The flowers are large in whorls of 4-6 on long, unbranched inflorescences. The corolla tube and upper lip are bluish violet with the upper lip slightly hairy and the lower lip pale bluish violet to white with the central lobe being paler, almost white.
It sets seed, but vegetative propagation is by division. It flowers in the first year from seed if sown in early spring. Hardy to -10°C.

Salvia sclarea *Linn.* 1753
Clary Sage

Native throughout Southern Europe & South-West & Central Asia.
This species is a hardy biennial or perennial. The large, broadly ovate, coarsely hairy leaves have notched to irregularly erose margins. They form a basal rosette in the first year, then later a clump to 2ft.(60cm) across. In the second year, the large, branched, pyramidal, inflorescences are formed on 4ft.(120cm) high coarsely hairy, stout stems from June to October. The flowers in whorls of 2-6 have a hooded, lilac/blue upper lip with a white lower lip surrounded by persistent and conspicuous, pinkish lilac, papery bracts which makes the plant so attractive. It is a very variable species which has given rise to the superior named form - S. sclarea var. turkestanica.

The whole plant is fetid and smells of ambergris and can often be smelt from a considerable distance, but this does not seem to put people off growing it, as it is one of the most popular species.
Propagation is usually by seed. The parent plant does not always die after flowering, but if it does there are usually seedlings around the plant to replace it.
Hardy to -10°C.

Salvia austriaca *Jacq.* 1774

Native to Eastern Europe from Czechoslovakia & Ukraine to North-East Bulgaria.
This is a hardy perennial dying back in winter. Hardy to at least -10°C.
The leaves are mostly basal, forming a rosette in the first year and enlarging to a clump 2ft.(60cm) across before sending up its flowering stems to a height of 3ft.(90cm) in the following June to September. The large leaves are dark green, ovate to elliptic, and coarsely and irregularly notched. The unbranched flowering stems have a few smaller leaves which are sessile (have no stems) and hold the long spikes of small, very pale, creamy yellow flowers with long exserted stamens.
Propagation is usually by seed, but vegetatively by division of the mature clump.
It is closely related to the following species

Salvia staminea *Montbr. & Auch. ex Benth.* 1836
syn. S. transcaucasica

Native to Asia Minor, East Turkey, Armenia, Georgia, & North & North-West Iran.
This is hardy perennial to 2½ x 1½ft.(75 x 45cm) dying back in winter. Hardy to at least -10°C.
The ovate to lanceolate leaves with notched margins form a basal rosette. The flowers which are white with purple spots in the throat, are in whorls of 2-6 from May to August on little branched stems with few stem leaves.

Salvia canescens *Mey*

Native to Caucasus.
This is a small, hardy perennial forming a small clump to 1½ x 1ft.(45 x 30cm) with mostly basal leaves which are elliptic to lanceolate and covered in dense, white, woolly hairs (hence the name canescens). The margins are irregularly notched giving the impression that they have been eaten. The flowers are violet purple, subtended by brownish purple, sticky bracts, from May to June with repeat flowering if pruned.

It is usually propagated by seed. Dormant in winter. Hardy to -10°C if not too wet.

Salvia candidissima *Vahl*   1804

Native to Greece, Albania, Turkey & Northern Iran.
This is another small, grey leaved perennial, frost hardy to -8°C, may be lower but dislikes too much rain. The leaves, which form a basal rosette to 1½ft.(45cm) across die down below ground in winter. They are ovate to lanceolate, with entire margins and covered in silky, white hairs. The flowering stems are to 2ft.(60cm) high from May to July with large, white flowers with a trace of yellow on the lower lip and the upper lip being hooded and flecked purple. Propagation is by seed or division.

Salvia frigida   *Boiss.*   1844

Native to Central & South-West Turkey & North-West Iran.
This is a similar hardy perennial to the above species, with leaves covered in silky, white hairs and forming a basal rosette which is dormant in winter. The flowers are a dull white to pale lilac in whorls of 2-6 on a single, branched inflorescence from May to July.

Salvia cyanescens   *Boiss. & Bal.*   1859

Native to Central Turkey.
This is a small perennial, frost hardy to at least -8°C, maybe lower, if given protection from the worst of our winter rain. The leaves are ovate to lanceolate, covered in masses of silky, white hairs and with entire to crenate margins. The basal leaves form a rosette in the first year and many branched inflorescences with few stem leaves appear from June to October in the following year, carrying pale blue/lilac flowers in whorls of 2-6 on long racemes to an overall height of 2½ft.(75cm). The upper lip is hooded and spotted with purple and the lower lip is flushed pale yellow. Dormant in winter. Propagation is by seed or division.

Salvia hypargeia   *Fisch. & Mey.*   1854

Native to Central, Southern & Eastern Turkey & Iran.
Mostly basal leaves form a small clump to 1 x 1ft.(30 x 30cm) which dies down in winter. The linear, greyish green leaves are felted above and covered in white, woolly hairs beneath. The margins are erose (irregularly notched as though they have been eaten), and often revolute (with the margins curled under) when young.
The unbranched flowering stems are produced the following year from June to September. The flowers are lavender blue, tinged purple with the upper lip hooded and the lower lip paler, almost white, whilst the calyx is covered in white, woolly, glandular hairs. Propagation is by seed or division. Hardy to -10°C if not too wet.

Salvia nutans *Linn.*   1753

Native to Central & Southern Russia, Crimea, Romania, Bulgaria, Siberia, Hungary & the Balkans.
This is hardy perennial that dies back in winter. The long, ovate to lanceolate leaves have very long petioles, are irregularly notched and form a clump to 2ft.(60cm). The thin, unbranched stems arise to 2ft.(60cm) with nodding racemes (hence nutans), at the tips containing close whorls of 4-7 small, pale blue flowers from June to October. Propagation is often by seed, but as it hybridises with close relatives, it should be propagated vegetatively by basal cuttings or layering.
Hardy to at least -10°C.

Salvia forskaohlei *Linn.*   1766

Native from South-East Europe to Western Asia including Bulgaria & the Black Sea coast of Turkey.
This is a hardy species, hardy to -15°C and dying back in winter.
The very large, broadly ovate leaves make a large clump to 3ft.(90cm) across. They are roughly hairy with notched margins. The large flowers are borne on large, branched inflorescences with a few smaller leaves to 3ft.(90cm) tall. The corolla tube is almost white, with a hooded upper lip and violet purple lower lip, with creamy yellow markings in the throat. This species is distinct because of the split upper lip.
Propagation is usually by seed, when it will flower by July from an early spring sowing and continue until October, but vegetative propagation is by division of the established clump.

Salvia viscosa *Jacq.*

Native to Italy.
This is a hardy perennial to 2 x 3ft(60 x 90cm). The basal leaves form a mound and the large, branched, sticky inflorescence (hence the name viscosa), has smaller stem leaves. The flowers are fairly small, with the upper lip being reddish pink and the lower lip being pale pink marked red and with a small, stickily hairy, reddish brown calyx. The flowering period is from June to October. Hardy to at least -10°C.
Propagation is usually by seed when plants will flower the same year, or vegetatively by division.

Salvia bulleyana *Diels.* 1912
syn. S. flava

Native to China & Yunnan.
It is a hardy perennial to 2 x 1½ft.(60 x 45cm) dying back in winter and hardy to at least -10°C. It benefits from partial shade and a soil that does not dry out too much in summer. The leaves are deep green, ovate to lanceolate and puckered similar to the foliage of beetroot with regularly crenate margins. They form a basal rosette in the first year.

The flowers from June to August of the following year are large, deep yellow with a maroon central lobe to the lower lip and in whorls of two usually on leafless, unbranched stems.

Propagation is by seed or division of an established clump.

Salvia japonica *Thunb.* 1784
syn. S. chinensis

Native to Japan, China & Korea.
This is half - hardy to tender perennial, which dies back in winter. It is a distinctive species with pinnate leaves with a terminal leaflet and two or three pairs of lateral leaves. They form a small clump to 1½ft(45cm) across, from which the almost leafless stems arise to a height of 2½ft.(75cm). The leaflets are deep green, veined purplish, ovate with dentate margins and surfaces almost glabrous. The flowers are small, pale lilac blue in whorls of 4 close together on the spike which is about 8in. (20cm) long from August to October. The upper lip is short and blunt and the lower lip is marked white within. Stamens are exserted. Hardy to about -4°C. Seed is produced but propagation is usually by cuttings.

Salvia przewalskii *Maxim.* 1881

Native to China & Sichuan.
This is a hardy perennial with basal leaves forming a clump to 3ft.(90cm) across and dying down below ground in winter. The leaves are ovate to lanceolate with long petioles and the margins regularly serrate, slightly pubescent above and covered in beige tomentum beneath. The large, maroon/purple flowers are in whorls of 2-4 in branched racemes held above the leaves to 3ft.(90cm) from June to August.
Propagation is by seed or division. Hardy to at least -15°C.

Salvia campanulata *Wallich. ex Benth.*

Native to the Himalayas from Northern India to South-West China.

This is a perennial, hardy to at least -10°C and dying back in winter forming a tuberous rootstock. It does best in partial shade and with a soil not too dry in summer. The leaves are very large, broadly ovate with regularly serrated margins, covered in soft, beige hairs above and with a thick, beige tomentum beneath, forming a basal clump in the first year to 2ft.(60cm) across. The following year the long, branched flowering stems to 2½ft.(75cm) carry the large, pale, creamy yellow flowers in whorls of 2-6 from May to August. The corolla tube is inflated with a small upper lip for the size of the overall flower.
Propagation is by seed or division of the mature clump.

Salvia castanea *Diels.* 1904

Native to the Himalayas in Western China, Bhutan, South-East Tibet, Northern Nepal & Yunnan.
This a half hardy perennial which dies down in winter. It is frost hardy to around -10°C but it is difficult to over winter as it often rots with too much rain. It also does not like to be too dry in summer. The leaves are ovate to lanceolate with serrate margins and long petioles, forming a basal clump to about 2ft.(60cm) across. The flowers from June to August the following year are a rich, deep maroon/purple, almost black, in whorls of 2-6 on inflorescences to 2ft.(60cm) tall. Propagation is by seed or vegetatively by division.

Group 2

Those species that are shrubby, with foliage either similar to the common sage, Salvia officinalis or pinnate foliage. Many of these have grey foliage and are early summer flowering with flowers sometimes produced intermittently thereafter. They are mostly hardy to -10°C and some will withstand lower temperatures if not too wet.

Salvia pomifera *Linn.*   1753
syn. S. calycina

Native to the Eastern Mediterranean including Western Turkey, Greece & Crete.
This is a moderately hardy, evergreen shrub to 3 x 3ft.(90 x 90cm). The bluish grey, strongly aromatic leaves are lanceolate to elliptic, rugose, pubescent below with margins crenate and undulate. The flowers are pale blue/lilac marked white, in whorls of 2-6, with persistent bracts on a paniculate inflorescence. The upper lip is almost straight, the calyx is reddish purple, glandular hairy, persistent, and enlarging in fruit. In its native habitat, wasps lay their eggs in the leaf axils and the plant secretes juices around them, forming galls.
Propagation is by seed or cuttings. Hardy to -10°C.

Salvia potentillifolia   *Boiss. & Heldr. ex Benth.*   1848

Native to Central & South-Western Turkey (endemic).
This is a half - hardy shrub to 2 x 2ft.(60 x 60cm) with foliage like potentilla, as its name implies. The leaves are small, grey, trisect or pinnatisect, with two pairs of lateral segments, all covered in white hairs, serrate at the tips and strongly aromatic. They are spread all over the erect stems, which are covered in long, white hairs above. The flowers are blue/lilac in whorls of 2-6 with a persistent, reddish brown calyx which expands in fruit. Propagation is by seed or cuttings. Frost hardy to around -10°C but dislikes winter wet.

Salvia candelabrum *Boiss.* 1838

Native to Spain.
This species is a hardy, woody, shrub to 3 x 3ft.(90 x 90cm). The stems are little branched, woody and stiff. The greyish green leaves are elliptic to lanceolate, rugose with crenate margins and stickily hairy and aromatic when crushed. The inflorescences are candelabra like - (hence the name) to 3ft.(90cm) tall, held high above the foliage, from June to September. The flowers are large, well spaced on the glabrous stems and have the unusual feature of being held vertically against the stem so that the lips point upwards. The corolla tube is white marked violet and the upper lip is pale violet with the lower lip rich, velvety purple with white markings. It is hardy to -10°C.
This species is often confused with S. ringens and S. interrupta which are similar in flower but have pinnate foliage.
Propagation is by seed or cuttings.

Salvia blancoana *Webb. & Heldr.* 1850

Native to Algeria, Morocco & South-East Spain.
This is a hardy, evergreen shrub for a warm, sunny position in poor, stony soil. It is often almost prostrate in habit to 1 x 2ft(30 x 60cm). The small, bluish grey leaves are elliptic to lanceolate, slightly rugose above and pubescent beneath with minutely crenate margins. Flowers are produced from May to July and intermittently thereafter. They are pale lilac/blue marked white in whorls of 2-6 on erect, slender, leafless stems.
Hardy to at least -10°C. Propagation is by seed or cuttings.

Salvia recognita *Fisch. & Mey.* 1854

Native to Turkey (endemic).
This is another hardy species forming a clump to 2 x 2ft.(60 x 60cm) with greyish, pinnate foliage with a large, ovate, terminal segment and three or four pairs of lateral leaflets with crenulate margins and covered in dense, white, glandular hairs. The large flowers are pale pink on large, branched inflorescences arising 3ft.(90cm) above the foliage from June to September. The upper lip is straight, not hooded and the lower lip has white markings.
Hardy to at least -10°C. Often dormant in winter. Propagation is by seed or cuttings.

Salvia ringens *Sibth. & Sm.* 1806

Native to Yugoslavia, Albania, Bulgaria, Romania and Greece. This is a bushy, hardy, evergreen shrub forming a mound of foliage to 2 x 2ft.(60 x 60cm) with inflorescences similar to S. candelabrum, also from June to September but with the flowers more bluish purple. The greyish green leaves are also pinnate with 2-3 pairs of small elliptical, pointed leaflets and softly hairy surfaces with crenate margins. It is hardy to -10°C in a dryish soil. Propagation is by seed or cuttings.

Salvia multicaulis *Vahl.* 1804
syn. S. acetabulosa

Native to South-West Asia, particularly Eastern, Central, & Southern Turkey.
This is a prostrate, spreading, evergreen shrublet forming mats to 2ft.(60cm) across. It is frost hardy to at least -10°C but it does not like it too wet. The leaves are similar to those of the common sage, S. officinalis, but more rounded, rugose and covered in grey tomentum above and below. The flowering stems are erect to1ft.(30cm) with whorls of 4-10 violet flowers enclosed within reddish brown calyces which are persistent, expanding and deepening in colour with formation of seed and subtended by reddish brown bracts. The main flowering period is May to June and often again in the autumn. Propagation is by seed, cuttings or layering.

Salvia jurisicii *Kosanin* 1770
Feathered Salvia

Native to Serbia & the Balkans.
This is a small half - hardy perennial to 1 x 1ft.(30 x 30cm), dying back in winter. The leaves are very unusual for a Salvia, being pinnate and almost fern like. The lateral leaflets are usually in 4-6 pairs with irregularly lobed margins and covered in fine, dense, white hairs. The flowers are small, pale lilac/blue and have the distinctive habit of hanging upside down in whorls of 2-7 on short, branched racemes from June to September.
Propagation is by seed or cuttings. It flowers the same year from seed. There is a white form S. jurisicii 'Alba' which must be propagated by cuttings to ensure white flowers. Hardy to -10°C, but does not like it too wet, although more tolerant than many species.

Salvia caespitosa *Montbr. & Auch. ex Benth.* 1836

Native to Central & Southern Turkey (endemic).
This species is a dwarf, evergreen shrub forming dense, prostrate mats as its name implies, to 9 x 12in.(22 x 30cm). It is reasonably frost hardy but needs protection from heavy rain. It is a good plant for a pot or the alpine house when it must be watered carefully so as not to wet the foliage, especially from autumn to spring. The small, grey leaves are pinnatisect with 2-4 pairs of lateral leaflets which have crenate margins and are covered in short, white hairs. The stems are also covered in long, soft hairs. The flowers are large, pinkish lilac in whorls of 2-6 in short terminal racemes, from May to July. The corolla tube is very wide and held up almost vertically and the lower lip is large and deflexed. Propagation can be by seed, cuttings or layering. Hardy to -10°C.

Salvia fruticosa *Mill.* 1768
syn S. triloba *Linn.* 1781

Native throughout the Mediterranean and Middle East including Algeria, Turkey, Lebanon, Israel, Palestine, Cyprus, Crete, Southern Italy, Sicily, Greece and the Canary Islands.

This is a hardy, evergreen shrub, hardy to at least -10°C, probably lower. It does not die down in the winter and does not get cut by the frost. The size after one season is 2½ x 2½ft.(75 x 75cm), but if left unpruned will spread to cover large areas. Fruticosa meaning shrubby is a better name for the plant than its synonym triloba, meaning with three lobed leaves. It is very variable, particularly in leaf as it is so widespread. We grow two forms; one with all simple leaves and one with some leaves three lobed.

The leaves are aromatic, pale green, elliptic to lanceolate, covered in soft, white hairs above and white tomentum below, with margins slightly crenate. Pale lilac pink flowers are produced in whorls of 2-8 on long spikes from May to July.

Propagation is by seed or cuttings.

Dried leaves are made into a tea and the fresh leaves infused with sugar or honey can be used to make a refreshing drink.

Salvia tomentosa *Mill.* 1768
syn. S. grandiflora

Native of Northern Europe to Western Asia including the Balkans, Crimea, Armenia, Turkey & Lebanon.

This is a hardy sub shrub to 2 x 3ft.(60 x 90cm). Hardy to -15°C.

The leaves are greyish green, rugose, narrowly oblong to ovate with margins minutely crenate or entire. The young leaves and stems are covered in dense, white tomentum hence the name. The fairly large flowers are lilac/blue, having a straight tube and upper lip whilst the lower lip is marked white. They are in whorls of 4-10 closely crowded on the stiff, erect, unbranched stems from June to October. Seed is produced in abundance, but vegetative propagation is from cuttings.

Salvia glutinosa *Linn.*   1753
Jupiters Distaff

Native to Central & Southern Europe from France & Spain in the west to Turkey & North & North-West Iran in the east.
This is a hardy perennial that inhabits moist places and deciduous forests, therefore a slightly moister soil and shady position are beneficial, although not absolutely necessary. It is hardy to at least -10°C and dies down below ground in winter.
It is a bushy perennial to 3 x 2ft.(90 x 60cm) with ovate to deltoid leaves with a distinctive sagittate (arrow shaped) base and covered in coarse hairs. The large, branched inflorescences are very sticky with long spikes of flowers to 18in.(45cm) long from July to November. The flowers are pale yellow with brownish red spots on the hooded upper lip with the lower lip being horizontal and striped brownish red.
It is a variable species with some forms having flowers that are nearly all yellow or with varying amounts of brownish red markings.

Salvia nubicola *Sweet*   1825

Native to Afghanistan, Kashmir, Nepal, Bhutan & Yunnan.
It is found at high altitudes, which is the meaning of the name nubicola. This is a similar species to S. glutinosa, forming a bushy perennial to 3 x 3ft.(90 x 90cm), but with thicker leaves and smaller flowers. The flowers also have the side lobes of the lower lip reflexed and a curved corolla tube.

Both species set seed but propagation is usually by cuttings.

The following species are from the Continent of Africa -

None of these species are hardy. They range from tender to half - hardy, but some seed around naturally which means that there is often a replacement if the parent plant dies. They are not particularly attractive or showy plants, the flowers usually being pale in colour. They all like a dryish, sandy soil in a sunny position.

Salvia africana - lutea *Linn.* 1762
syn. S. aurea

Native to South Africa.
This is small, half - hardy to tender shrub of stiff, much branched habit to 2½ x 2½ft.(75 x 75cm). Hardy to -4°C. The leaves are pale green, pungently aromatic, rounded in outline with undulate, entire margins often with irregular lobing at the base. They are covered in minute, white hairs above and on the veins below. The stems are woody below and covered in white tomentum above. The flowers are not freely produced in this country but will appear at any time from June to October. in whorls of two in short terminal racemes. They are large, yellow flowers which soon fade to brown, with a hooded upper lip, with persistent, green calyces which expand and turn brownish red in fruit.
The leaves are used to make a tea and it is also known as a diaphoretic (perspiration inducing drug). Seed are sometimes produced but propagation is usually by cuttings.

Salvia lanceolata *Lam.* 1791

Native to South Africa.
This species is similar in appearance to the previous species, but it produces more flowers over a period from July to September.
It is a half - hardy to tender shrub to 2½ x 2ft.(75 x 60cm) with a stiff branching habit. The leaves are small, grey and lanceolate, as its name implies and glabrous, with entire margins. The large, hooded flowers emerge yellow and soon turn a fabulous dusky pink.
Propagation is again by seed or cuttings. Probably hardy to around -4°C.

Salvia repens *Burch. ex Benth.* 1833
Creeping Sage

Native to South Africa.
This is a half - hardy perennial spreading by means of the creeping, woody rhizome to 2 x 3ft.(60 x 90cm). The lanceolate leaves, aromatic when bruised are coarse with serrate margins. The corolla tube and upper lip are a pale lilac blue and the lower lip is white with lilac blue markings. The long racemes of flowers are produced from June to August. Propagation is by seed or cuttings. Hardy to -5°C but seedlings are usually produced around the plant in profusion. It has many herbal and medicinal uses in its native areas. It was also at one time used as an incense and smoked by the local tribesmen.

Salvia stenophylla *Burch. ex Benth.* 1833

Native to South Africa.
This is a similar half - hardy perennial to the above species but having smaller, lanceolate to lyrate leaves with deep and irregular lobing and crenate margins. The flowers are also smaller.

Salvia scabra *Thunb.* 1781

Native to South Africa.
This is a small, tender perennial to 2 x 2ft.(60 x 60cm) with a stiff, branched habit, woody at the base with small, ovate, leaves with serrated margins. The stems, leaves and calyces are all covered in rough hairs, hence the name scabra. The fairly large flowers are an attractive pale lilac/pink with a long, narrow corolla tube and a short, straight upper lip with a divided middle lobe of the lower lip. It flowers almost continuously from July to October. It is used medicinally in its native country. Propagation is by seed or cuttings. Hardy to -3°C.

Salvia africana - caerulea *Linn.*   1753

Native to South Africa.
This is a half - hardy to tender species with a well branched, bushy habit to 4 x 3ft.(120 x 90cm).
The leaves are small, elliptic and leathery, greyish green above and white tomentose beneath, either entire or slightly serrate, often lobed at the base. The bracts and calyces are persistent. The calyx is green tinged brown around the edges, enlarging and turning more reddish brown when the flowers have fallen. The pale lilac/blue flowers are in whorls of 2-6 on 6in.(15cm) long racemes from July to November. The upper lip is slightly hairy and a deeper colour, whilst the lower lip is beautifully marked with white.
Propagation is by seed or cuttings. Hardy to -4°C.
It has many medicinal uses and is known as a diaphoretic (a medicine which promotes perspiration).

Salvia taraxacifolia *Coss. & Bal. ex Hook.*   1872

Native to the Atlas Mountains of Morocco.

This is a small, half - hardy to tender perennial, being a very attractive small plant, suitable for the rockery. In cold areas, it is best treated as an annual. It looks good even when not in flower, due to the thistle like rosettes of leaves to 1ft.(30cm) across, which are lyrate to pinnate, hence the name taraxacifolia, meaning with leaves like the Taraxium family, of which the dandelion is a member. It does not however look like a dandelion, as the leaflets are ovate to elliptic with margins sharply serrate and undulate, dark green covered in white hairs above and white pubescence beneath. The flowering stems, with a few smaller leaves, reach 2ft.(60cm) with large, pale pink flowers in unbranched racemes. The hooded upper lip is pale pink and covered in dense, white hairs, whilst the lower lip is slightly deeper in colour and marked white within. The bracts and calyces are persistent, with long spines, and with the calyces being covered in long, white hairs giving a silvery appearance. This species has no close relations.

Propagation is by seed or division. Hardy to about -3°C.

Salvia tingitana *Etlinger* 1777
syn. S. foetida

Native to Northern Morocco, particularly the area around Tangiers, hence the name tingitana.
The synonym of foetida is due to the very strongly but pleasantly aromatic foliage.

This is a tender, bushy perennial to 3 x 3ft.(90 x 90cm) closely related to S. sclarea. The pale green leaves are ovate to almost heart shaped, thin and wrinkled and sparsely covered in long, fine, white hairs above and on the veins below and with the margins irregularly notched to lobed. The inflorescences are branched with flower spikes to 6in.(15cm) long from June to October. The corolla tube is white with a hooded, pale lilac upper lip and side lobes of the lower lip, with the mid lobe being creamy yellow and cup shaped. The stamens are exserted.
Propagation is by seed or cuttings. Hardy to around -3°C.

Salvia algeriensis *Desf.* 1798

Native to Morocco and Algeria, hence the name algeriensis.
This is an annual species making a bushy plant to 2 x 2ft.(60 x 60cm). Plants from seed sown in early spring will be in flower by mid summer and continue flowering prolifically until the end of October, but propagation can also be from cuttings. The flowers on branched racemes are large with the short corolla tube being almost white and the hooded, upper lip and almost horizontal lower lip being pale violet blue with the upper lip covered in violet hairs at the tip and the mid lobe of the lower lip being cup shaped.

The following two species are endemic to the Canary Islands but are completely different from each other and from the previous group of species.

Salvia broussonetii *Benth.* 1833
syn. S. bolleana

This is tender perennial with a well branched, mound forming habit to 3 x 3ft.(90 x 90cm). The large, aromatic, pale green leaves are ovate to heart shaped with irregularly notched margins and covered in white, glandular hairs particularly beneath, making them quite sticky.
The shyly produced, branched inflorescences bear whorls of 2-6 hooded, pure white flowers, subtended by green bracts, at any time between June and October. The calyx is covered in dense, sticky, glandular hairs, the same as the leaves.
Propagation is by seed or cuttings. Hardy to about -3°C.

Salvia canariensis *Linn.* 1753

This is a half - hardy to tender perennial with a bushy habit to 4 x 3ft.(120 x 90cm). It occasionally survives temperatures as low as -5 or -6°C.

The young stems are covered in dense, white tomentum. The oblong leaves with a hastate base are a greyish green, covered in short, white hairs, and with either entire or slightly crenate margins. The flowers are in short, branched racemes with whorls of 4-8 fls, being pale lilac/pink with the upper lip hooded and lower lip marked white. The thin, papery calyces and bracts are persistent, green tinged lilac pink, turning more colourful with age and being particularly attractive after the flowers have fallen, giving the effect that the plant is still in flower.

Seed is produced, but propagation is usually by cuttings.

Group 3

Hardy bushy, perennials, with leaves spread all over the stems, flowering throughout most of the summer, beginning in May or June.

Salvia verticillata *Linn.* 1753

Native to most of Europe including Caucasus, Northern Iran, Iraq & Turkey.
This is a hardy perennial to 2½ x 2½ft.(75 x 75cm) which usually seeds around and dies back below ground in winter. The ovate to triangular leaves with margins almost entire to notched, often have one or two pairs of unequal basal leaves. The small, violet blue flowers are closely packed in dense, globular whorls of 20-40 on branched racemes. The calyx is tinged purplish and is attractive and persistent after the flowers have fallen. If the flowering stems are cut back after flowering it will give repeat successions of flower from June to October. Hardy to -15°C.

This is a very variable species usually propagated by seed. However it needs to be propagated by cuttings to come true, particularly the named cultivars such as -

S. verticillata 'Purple Rain'
a form with deeper purple calyces and flowers.

S. verticillata 'Alba' - (see photo) which will not always have white flowers when grown from seed.

S. verticillata subsp. amasiaca
lower growing to 1½ft.(45cm) and little branched.

Salvia virgata *Jacq.* 1770
syn. S. sibthorpii

Native to the Eastern Mediterranean to Central Asia including Crimea, the Balkans, Italy, Caucasus, Iran, Northern Iraq & Afghanistan.
This is a hardy perennial closely related to S. nemorosa but with a more branched and open habit and with fewer stem leaves, similar to S. dichroantha to which it is also closely related but shorter to 2ft.(60cm). The leaves are ovate to lanceolate with crenate margins. The flowers are deep violet from June to October. The corolla tube hardly protrudes from the calyx but has a hooded upper lip. Propagation is by seed when it will flower the same year, or cuttings. Hardy to -15°C. Often dormant in winter.

Salvia nemorosa *Linn.* 1762

Native to Central Europe, Eastern Turkey, the Balkans, Southern & Central Russia, Crimea, Caucasus, Iran & Afghanistan.

This is a hardy species, to -15°C with erect branching habit to 2½ x 2ft.(75 x 60cm). The leaves are ovate to lanceolate with crenulate margins. The small flowers are violet purple with many in each whorl which are close together on the stems in erect, terminal spikes.

There are many named forms of S. nemorosa, which unless they are propagated vegetatively, cannot be called by the cultivar name.

'East Friesland'	-	shorter, compact habit
'Lubecca'	-	shorter, compact habit
'Rose Queen'	-	pink flowers
'Wesuwe'	-	dwarf, deep purple fls.
'Amethyst'	-	violet flowers (see photo)

Propagation is often by seed, but it hybridises readily with similar species, which has given rise to the following hybrids -

S. x superba   = S. nemorosa x virgata
S. x sylvestris = S. pratensis x nemorosa
S. x sylvestris 'Blauhugel' - has deep blue flowers with no trace of purple

Salvia amplexicaulis *Lam.* 1791
syn. S. villicaulis

Native to Hungary and the Balkans.

This is a bushy, hardy perennial to 3 x 3ft.(90 x 90cm) with a branched, compact habit. It is closely related to S. nemorosa but is more hairy. The hairy leaves are ovate to lanceolate and sessile, clasping the hairy stems (hence the name amplexicaulis). The flowers are violet blue with a hooded upper lip covered in fine hairs and the lower lip is well divided into three lobes with the mid lobe being cup shaped. The whorls of many flowers are close together to form almost a continuous spike. Hardy to -15°C. Dormant in winter.

Propagation is by seed or cuttings.

The New World

This section consists of 500 species of which the majority, 312 species are from Mexico with 88% being endemic. Salvias can here again be divided into three groups.

Group 1

Those from the USA excluding Mexico. Many of these are plants from the arid areas of California. They are difficult to grow in our climate as it is too wet and not sunny and warm enough. They can be planted out as annuals for foliage effect but they are difficult to get into flower. In their native areas, their normal flowering period is in the spring and early summer after the winter rain. They finish flowering and go dormant when it gets really dry and hot in the summer. Typically they are large shrubs with grey, strongly aromatic, often camphorous foliage and large glomerules of many small, pale flowers. They hybridise readily with each other.

Salvia mellifera *Greene* 1892
Black Sage

Native to South-West California in the low foothills of the mountains.
In this country this species is a half - hardy to tender shrub to 4 x 3ft.(120 x 90cm). The stems are branched and woody at the base. The strongly aromatic leaves are lanceolate to oblong, leathery, rugose, almost glabrous above and covered with white tomentum beneath. The flowers are small and pale lavender blue, almost white with many flowers tightly packed together forming a glomerule of which there are several on each stem. Mature plants flower with us in the spring in the greenhouse and then continue when planted outside into early summer. It is a good honey plant, as the whole plant is fragrant and attractive to bees. The name mellifera means honey bearing. It also yields an essential oil which smells of camphor. The leaves can be dried and used in the same way as the common sage, as a tea and as a seasoning. Propagation is by seed or cuttings. Hardy to about -4°C.

Salvia clevelandii *Greene* 1892
San Diego or Blue Sage

Native to a small area of California, east of San Diego.
The foliage is very similar to the above species, although botanically it is placed in a different section because of the flower structure which is more similar to the next two species. It is smaller then S. mellifera to 3 x 3ft.(90 x 90cm) with greyer, highly aromatic foliage. The flowers are violet blue, slightly larger with less to a whorl and usually only one capitate whorl to each stem of the branched inflorescence.

Salvia apiana *Jepson*   1908
White Sage

Native to South-West California along the coast from Santa Barbara County to Los Angeles, where it grows to 7 or 8ft. (210 - 240cm). Here it is a tender shrub to about 3 x 2ft.(90 x 60cm). It will not usually over winter outside as it is too wet, although it may be frost hardy to about -3°C if dry. The stems, leaves and calyces are covered in minute, flattened, white hairs giving the whole plant a white appearance, hence the name. The strongly aromatic leaves are elliptic to lanceolate with entire margins. The flowering stems are mainly leafless and branched forming a tall, pyramidal, thysoidal inflorescence (with the side branches very erect and close to the central stem). The flowers are few in loose whorls, white to pale lilac or flecked lilac.
Propagation is by seed or cuttings, although seed is unlikely to set in the UK.

Salvia leucophylla *Greene*   1892
Chaparral Sage

Native to South-West California around Santa Barbara, San Bernadino & Los Angeles where it grows to a height of 6ft.(180cm). In this country it is a small, tender shrub with an erect habit to 3 x 2ft.(90 x 60cm). The leaves are lanceolate to oblong, blunt at the tip, with crenulate margins, pale grey, tomentose above and white beneath. The flowers are pinkish lilac to purple in compact whorls subtended by white, tomentose bracts on stout spikes. It is difficult to over winter here because of the wet and damp atmosphere. Hardy to -3°C. Propagation is by seed or cuttings.

Salvia carduacea *Benth.*   1833
Thistle Sage

Native to Southern California.
This is a very attractive annual species to 1½ x 1ft.(45 x 30cm) with aromatic, thistle like leaves , elliptic in outline, pinnatifid with lobed and spiny toothed margins forming a basal rosette. The usually single stem is erect and leafless. The flowers are from June to August or earlier in its native habitat, numerous in close, globular whorls (a glomerule) surrounded by reflexed bracts. The upper lip is violet, ragged at the tips with the middle lobe of the lower lip widely spreading. The calyx is covered in long, spiny hairs. It is propagated by seed, when it will flower the same year.

Salvia columbariae *Benth.* 1833
Chia

Native to California, Arizona & New Mexico.

This is another annual with a similar habit and attractive, but completely different foliage to the previous species. It has grey, basal leaves forming a rosette to 1½ x 1ft.(45 x 30cm) which are oblong to ovate in outline, deeply pinnatifid with crenate or lobed margins, and a bullate surface covered in long hairs.

The usually single stem has one or two pairs of smaller leaves and carries large, globular heads densely packed with numerous, very small, pale blue flowers with glandular, hairy calyces. It is a very attractive small plant.

This plant has medicinal properties and a tea is made with an infusion of the leaves. It is one of several species producing seeds known as Chia, which are rich in mucilage and oil, having high energy values and thirst quenching properties. They are harvested by the local people and can be ground and added to food.

Salvia spathacea *Greene* 1892
Pitcher Sage or Humming Bird Sage

Native to California and restricted to the extreme South-West coastal plains.

This is an interesting and very attractive species with large, showy flowers but with only a few open at any time. It does well in partial shade. It is hardy to -10°C when established and not too wet. It spreads underground by means of creeping rhizomes and will form low, ground covering mounds to 1 x 3ft.(30 x 90cm). It dies back below ground in winter. The leaves are oblong with a hastate base and together with the stems are covered in sticky hairs. The leaves are close together hugging the stem forming a spathe, hence the name spathacea and the  upper leaves are sessile. The stout inflorescence arises above the leaves to 3ft.(90cm). The flowers are in well spaced, globular whorls of 2-20, subtended by numerous, sticky bracts. The flowers are deep, rose pink with a long corolla tube, short, blunt upper lip, vertical lower lip, exserted stamens and a stickily, hairy calyx. Propagation is by seed or basal cuttings.

Group 2

Those from the USA states of Texas, Arizona & New Mexico and continuing into Mexico. These are small to medium, bushy plants, often shrubs, with small leaves spread all over the plants. They are usually half - hardy in our climate, with a long flowering season beginning in July. The best known of this type is probably -

Salvia greggii *Gray* 1870

Native to North-East & Central Mexico & Texas.
This is a small shrub to 2½ x 2½ft.(75 x 75cm). The leaves are small, elliptic, glabrous and leathery with entire margins. It flowers prolifically from July to November or even later if mild. The flowers are a mauvish red in whorls of two. It is hardy to -6°C.

S. greggii 'Peach'

Forms of S. greggii with different colour flowers are -

'Alba'	-	flowers white
'Peach'	-	flowers peachy/orange
'Raspberry Royal'	-	flowers purplish red
'Keter's Red'	-	flowers orange/red
'La Encantada'	-	flowers reddish pink

They occasionally set seed, but to ensure plants are true they should be propagated by cuttings as they hybridise readily with the following species, S. microphylla. This has given rise to many named hybrids of greggii and microphylla named by James Compton as S. x jamensis (pronounced hamensis) after the village of Jame in Mexico, near where some of these forms were found in the wild by Compton, Darcy & Rix in 1991.

Some of the named forms of **S. x jamensis** are -

'Los Lirios'	-	orange/red	**'Fuego'**	-	orange
'La Tarde'	-	pink	**'Pat Vlasto'**	-	peachy/orange
'La Siesta'	-	pink	**'Devantville'**	-	orange
'La Luna'	-	pale yellow	**'James Compton'**	-	deep crimson
'El Duranzo'	-	orange/red			

Salvia greggii x lycioides

This a half - hardy small shrub with a lax, spreading habit to 1½ x 1½ft.(45 x 45cm). It is hardier than greggii to -10°C, even though it is more delicate looking with its tiny leaves and thin stems. It does well in a slightly shady position. The leaves are smaller than S. greggii, elliptic to lanceolate, glabrous and leathery with entire margins. The flowers are slightly smaller than greggii but a lovely, bright reddish purple with a deep purple calyx usually in whorls of 2 from July to November or later.

It sets seed freely and although it will usually come true, vegetative propagation should be by cuttings.

Salvia microphylla *HBK.* 1817
syn. S. grahamii
Myrtle Salvia

Native to Central Mexico, New Mexico & Arizona.

This is a half - hardy, woody shrub to 4 x 4ft.(120 x 120cm). The leaves are pale green, ovate to elliptic, larger than the above species, slightly hairy and with serrated margins. They smell of blackcurrants when crushed. The flowers are bright red in whorls of 2-4, larger than S. greggii with a hooded upper lip and longer, widely spreading lower lip which is almost horizontal. It flowers from July to November or even later. It usually gets caught by the frost with us, but if it does not it will get larger each year and may benefit by being pruned in the spring. It is hardy to -10°C but not without some damage.

It sets seed, but as it hybridizes readily with S. greggii it should be propagated by cuttings.

Cultivars of **S. microphylla** -
- **'Pink Blush'** - a form with pink flowers.
- **'Newby Hall'** - very similar to the species but larger to 6ft.(180cm) tall.
- **'La Foux'** - similar to 'Newby Hall' but with blackish calyces.
- **'Cerro Potosi'** - collected in the wild from the mountain of the same name, magenta flowers.
- **'Oxford'** - small, triangular leaves and deep crimson flowers.
- **'Ruth Stungo'** - a sport of 'Oxford' with variegated foliage.

Salvia microphylla var. neurepia   *(Fern.) Epling*   1939
syn. S. neurepia

Native to Central Mexico, particularly San Luis Potosi State.
A variety of S. microphylla and often confused with it, but it is a slightly larger, more vigorous plant with slightly larger flowers and shiny, glabrous leaves which is the most distinguishing feature. Hardy to -10°C.

Salvia microphylla var. wislizenii   *Gray*   1886
syn. S. lemmonii

Native to Mexico, Arizona and New Mexico.
A variety of S. microphylla with deep, rose pink flowers in a more erect, condensed raceme and with shiny, deep green leaves, more triangular in shape and pointed at the tip. It is also deciduous. Hardy to -10°C.

Salvia microphylla subsp. microphylla

Native to Mexico.
This is a more spreading shrub to 2½ x 3ft.(75 x 90cm). It is smaller in all its parts than S. microphylla, with flowers a deeper, more purplish red. Hardy to -10°C.

Salvia chamaedryoides   *Cav.*   1793
syn. S. chamaedryfolia
Germander Sage

Native to Texas & North & Central Mexico.
This is a half - hardy shrub similar to S. greggii and S. microphylla at first glance, but with a more sprawling habit; hence the name chamaedryoides, meaning ground hugging. The flowers, however, are a deep blue in whorls of 4-6. The upper lip is small and pubescent and the lower lip is flared, horizontal with white markings in the throat. The leaves are small, greyish green covered in fine hairs, elliptic to obovate with margins elliptic to finely crenate.
S. chamaedryoides var. isochroma from the arid mountain areas of San Luis Potosi state of Mexico, has smaller, greyer leaves, smaller flowers and a more upright habit. Propagation is by seed or cuttings. Hardy to -6°C.

Salvia arizonica *Gray* 1886

Native to New Mexico and Arizona.
This is a half-hardy perennial to 2½ x 2ft.(75 x 60cm) with a dense, compact habit. The small, dainty, triangular leaves are glabrous with regularly serrate margins. The flowers are small, mid blue in whorls of 6-8 from July to October, with a short upper lip covered with short, white hairs and a larger, deeper blue lower lip. Dormant in winter. Hardy to at least -6°C. Propagation is by seed or cuttings.

The following species is completely different from the previous group of species, and with no near relatives in these areas; the nearest relations being in Northern USA and others being in Asia and Africa.

Salvia roemeriana *Scheele* 1849
Cedar Sage

Native to Texas, Arizona and North-East Mexico.
This is a small, tender perennial, best grown as an annual. It is a dainty plant to 1 x 1ft.(30 x 30cm) suitable for growing in a pot, with rounded leaves with dentate margins which are slightly undulate. The flowers are bright scarlet in loose racemes from July to October.
The corolla tube is long and narrow with small lips. Hardy to -3°C. Propagation is by seed or cuttings and those grown from seed flower within a few months.

The following two species from the USA are not related to the previous group and are completely different to them and from each other.

Salvia azurea *Mich. ex Lam.* 1792

Native to South-East USA including Arkansas, Kentucky & Texas.

This is a half - hardy to tender perennial, dying back in winter, with an erect, habit to 5ft.(150cm) with stems mostly unbranched except for short, side branches. Due to the lax, floppy habit of this plant it either needs staking or planting in a small gap to be supported between other plants. The leaves, are linear to lanceolate, downy above with margins minutely serrate and ciliate (with hairs round the edges). The flowers are azure blue as you would expect from the name, in whorls of 3-6 in short, dense racemes from August to November. The upper lip is short and blunt with the lower lip being larger, flared horizontal and marked white. The form more often seen in cultivation is **S. azurea subsp. Pitcheri** which comes from Mexico and is only hardy to around -3°C. Seed is sometimes produced but propagation is usually by cuttings.

Salvia lyrata *Linn.*
Cancer Weed

Native to East USA particularly North Carolina.

The name Cancer Weed refers to its supposed healing properties and not for causing cancer. It is a half - hardy to tender perennial which seeds around a little so that there is usually a plant to replace the parent if it dies. In cold areas, it is best treated as an annual. The leaves are fairly large, lyrate in shape, hence the name, deep green, edged and veined deep maroon and forming a very attractive basal rosette 1ft.(30cm) across. If in full sun and dry conditions the leaves often turn practically all maroon. The stem leaves are few and smaller, lyrate to pinnatifid with edges undulate to lobed. The flower stems are erect, to 1½ft.(45cm) tall, sparsely branched, deep maroon and covered in white hairs. Small, insignificant, violet flowers in whorls of 3-10 are produced from June to October. In my experience the first flowers of the season usually protrude from the calyx, but the following successions of flowers are cleistogamous (flowers are formed inside the calyx, but not displayed, yet seed is set.). The calyx is green marked reddish brown and with bristly teeth. This is an interesting and distinct species, attractive for the foliage alone. Propagation is by seed or vegetatively by division. Hardy to around -3°C.

Group 3

Those from the more tropical areas of Mexico and Central and Southern America. Mostly large, mostly tender, bushy perennials, best grown as annuals in our climate, flowering from July onwards, with bright, colourful flowers mostly in shades of red or blue, often grown in forest or shady conditions in their native habitat, therefore requiring more humus in the soil and requiring water in very hot, dry periods. They usually do not set seed in our climate.

Salvia concolor *Lam. ex Benth.* 1833
syn. S. cyanea

Native to Mexico.
This is a half - hardy perennial to 6ft.(180cm) tall. The stems are hollow and tinged blue at the nodes and it benefits from partial shade and a position where it is not too dry, as in its native habitat it grows on wooded slopes by the side of streams. The pale green leaves are large, ovate to heart shaped, thin and coarsely serrated. The large flowers are uniformly deep, bright blue with calyces to match, in whorls of 6-10 with no trace of varying colour or markings, hence the name concolor, from July to November or later if mild. Seed is not usually produced. Propagation is by cuttings. Dormant in winter. Hardy to -8°C, maybe lower.

Salvia leucantha *Cav.* 1791

Native to East Central Mexico & tropical Central & South America.
This is a tender shrub to 3 x 3ft.(90 x 90cm). The stems are woody below and covered in dense, white tomentum above. The grey, lanceolate leaves, which smell of blackcurrant when crushed, are rugose and covered in white hairs above and dense, white tomentum below. The

flowers are in whorls of 6-8, being covered in a dense, white, woolly down with a straight corolla and short, blunt lips. The calyx is very showy, being covered in dense, mauve, woolly down. There is also a form with the calyx and corolla both mauve. It will often begin flowering in June with us, but occasionally as late as August and will continue until November or the frosts.
This plant never sets seed here. Propagation is by cuttings. Hardy to -4°C.

Saliva blepharophylla *Brand. ex Epling* 1930

Native to Mexico.

This species is a half - hardy perennial to 1½ x 3ft.(45 x 90cm), spreading by means of fleshy, underground stolens, and dying back in winter. The leaves are ovate, deep, dull green and glabrous with serrate and ciliate (fringed with hairs) margins. The species name means - fringed like eyelashes.

The flowers, which are produced from June to November are large, bright orange/red in whorls of 2-6 on short, unbranched racemes, with the upper lip being covered in very fine, dense hairs of the same colour, giving a velvety appearance. It does not usually set seed therefore propagation is by cuttings. Hardy to at least -8°C.

A similar species which originated in Mexico, but is not known in the wild -

Salvia buchananii *Hedge* 1963
syn. S. bacheriana

This is a small, tender evergreen, suitable for growing in a pot as it only reaches 1 x 1ft.(30 x 30cm). It spreads very slightly by means of its fleshy rhizomes.

The ovate to lanceolate leaves are a distinctive dark green, leathery and glossy and with crenate margins. The flowers are the same as the above species, large and covered in dense, velvety hairs, but in a bright cerise colour from June to October in whorls of 3-6. The calyx and stems are purplish brown.

It does not set seed, therefore propagation is by cuttings. Hardy to -3°C.

Salvia discolor *HBK.* 1818

Native to Peru.
This is a tender perennial with a lax habit to 2 x 3ft.(60 x 90cm). Hardy to only -2°C. The leaves are pale green, leathery, ovate to lanceolate with entire margins. The undersides of the leaves and the stems are covered in dense, white tomentum, but the long, drooping flower stems are yellowish green and very sticky, with whorls of 3-9 deep indigo purple, almost black flowers just peeping out from the calyx, which is pale green and covered in dense, white hairs.

It is a plant that is best viewed from below as in a hanging basket.

It never sets seed in our climate and propagation is by cuttings.

Salvia oppositiflora *Ruiz. & Pav.* 1798

Native to Peru.
This is a tender perennial with a spreading habit to 1½ x 3ft.(45 x 90cm). It is one of the most frost sensitive species, being only hardy to -2°C. The pale green leaves are ovate to cordate, hairy beneath and with undulate, serrate margins.

The flowers are bright orange from June to November, in pairs on short, unbranched racemes. They have a long corolla tube together with the upper lip covered in white hairs, the lower lip curved upwards and exserted stamens.

It never sets seed in our climate and propagation is by cuttings.

Salvia patens *Cav.* 1799

Native to Central Mexico.

S. patens 'Guanajuato'

This is a tender to half - hardy perennial to 2½ x 2ft.(75 x 60cm) with variable hardiness, which dies down to its tuberous roots in winter. We have known it to survive a wet winter with temperatures of -7°C but to die in a drier winter when temperatures only dropped to -6°C. The leaves are narrowly triangular, with a hastate base, pubescent on both surfaces and with margins regularly notched. The flowers are very large with a short corolla tube, large, hooded upper lip and large lower lip, both of which are softly pubescent. The species is deep, royal blue in whorls of 2 well spaced on the long flowering stems from July to October. In

very hot summers it does not flower so well. To over winter young plants in the glasshouse, cuttings should be taken slightly earlier than with other species in order for the tuberous roots to become established to survive the winter. It can also be grown from seed which usually comes true but cannot be guaranteed.

S. patens 'Chilcombe'

S. patens 'Cambridge Blue' - flowers paler blue
    'Chilcombe' - flowers lavender blue
    'White Trophy' - flowers white
    'Guanajuato' - a larger form, with even larger flowers of the same colour as the species and leaves often blotched brown, found in the Sierra de Guanajuato by Compton, Darcy & Rix in 1991.

Salvia sinaloensis *Fern.* 1900

Native to North-West Mexico, particularly Sinaloa, hence the name.
This is small, tender perennial to 1 x 1ft.(30 x 30cm) with small, elliptic, leaves tinged purplish red above to almost completely purplish red beneath, sparsely hairy with margins entire to slightly serrate and often lightly ciliate (fringed with hairs). The flowers are in whorls of 2-3, from July to October, being deep, bright blue with a small, hooded upper lip and a horizontal, spreading lower lip marked white within.
It does well in a pot, where the amount of water it receives can be more carefully controlled, as it is particularly prone to damping off or dying for no apparent reason particularly in the winter. Therefore it should be watered very sparingly from autumn to spring, taking care not to get the foliage wet.
Propagation is by cuttings. Hardy to -3°C. It is well worth persevering with as the foliage and flowers are a striking contrast.

Salvia elegans *Vahl.* 1804
syn. S. incarnata
Pineapple Sage or Honey Melon Sage

Native to Central Mexico and Guatemala.
This is a half - hardy perennial of compact, dense, bushy habit to 3 x 3ft.(90 x 90cm). It dies back in winter and is hardy to at least -6°C. but will still begin flowering in June and continue through to November. The leaves are ovate to heart shaped, covered in fine, soft hairs, slightly pineapple scented

and with regularly serrate margins. The flowers are bright scarlet with a long, narrow corolla tube in whorls of 2-6 in loose panicles. Propagation is by cuttings.

Salvia elegans 'Scarlet Pineapple'
syn. S. rutilans
Pineapple Sage

This is the true pineapple sage, which until recently was known as S. rutilans. It is a tender perennial to 4 x 4ft.(120 x 120cm) and it is only hardy to -3°C. The leaves are lanceolate, softly hairy and strongly pineapple scented. It is also much later flowering than the above species, from October onwards, although the flowers are the same. There is also a form with paler, salmon pink flowers known as S. elegans 'Frieda Dixon'.

Salvia guaranitica *St. Hil. ex Benth.* 1833
syn. S. caerulea
syn. S. ambigens

Native to Brazil, Argentina, Paraguay & Uruguay.
This is half - hardy perennial to 4ft.(120cm), spreading by means of underground tubers, and dying back in winter. It does best in a partially shaded, not too dry position. The leaves are similar to those of the stinging nettle, ovate, deep green, roughly hairy with serrated margins.
The flowers are large, deep blue from July to November, in whorls of 2-8 on long unbranched racemes. Hardy to -10°C. Propagation is by cuttings.

There are several named forms of this species around, the most common being -

Salvia guaranitica 'Black & Blue' *Compton* 1987

This is a taller plant to 7ft.(210cm). with deeper, more purplish blue flowers which are much later, from October onwards and with deep blue almost black calyces from whence it gets its name. Hardy only to -4°C.
S. guaranitica 'Argentine Skies' has pale, sky blue flowers.

Salvia mexicana *Linn.* 1753

Native to Central & Southern Mexico.
This is a similar species to the above, a tender perennial to 6ft.(180cm) with ovate, greyish green leaves and deep blue flowers from November onwards. Hardy to only about -2°C. Propagation is by cuttings.

The form more commonly seen in cultivation is -

Salvia mexicana var. minor *Benth.* 1848

This is a form to 5ft.(150cm) with deep, bluish green, ovate leaves and small, bright blue flowers with lime green calyces from July to November or later if mild. Propagation is by cuttings. Hardy to -3°C.

Salvia fulgens *Cav.* 1791
syn. S. cardinalis
Cardinal Sage

Native to Central Mexico.
This is a tender perennial to 5ft.(150cm). The leaves are ovate, softly hairy above with crenate margins. The large, bright scarlet flowers are in whorls of 2-6 on long unbranched spikes, from July to November, with a brownish red calyx and the corolla tube and upper lip being covered in dense, soft hairs giving a velvety appearance. Propagation is by cuttings. Hardy to -4°C.

Salvia gesneraeflora *Lindl. & Paxton* 1851

Native to Mexico & Colombia.
This is a tender, bushy shrub to 4 x 4ft.(120 x 120cm). It is very similar to S. fulgens but with even larger, scarlet flowers and larger, more broadly ovate leaves. It will not flower outside here, but with us it flowers in the early spring under glass. Propagation is by cuttings. Hardy to -3°C.

Salvia 'Purple Majesty'

This is an hybrid between S. guaranitica and S. gesneraeflora which occurred at Huntingdon Botanic Garden in California.

It is a tender perennial to 5ft.(150cm) tall and only hardy to around -4°C.
The foliage most closely resembles that of S. guaranitica and the large, purple flowers are borne from August to November.

Propagation is by cuttings.

Salvia amarissima *Ortega* 1797

Native to Mexico.
This is a vigorous, bushy, tender shrub to 3 x 3ft.(90 x 90cm). The deep green, ovate to triangular leaves are covered in sticky hairs on both surfaces. The flowers are fairly small, mid blue with a small, closed upper lip and a larger, flared horizontal, lower lip in whorls of 6 from July to October. It occasionally sets seed, but propagation is usually by cuttings. Hardy to -3°C.

Salvia urica *Epling* 1939

Native to Mexico, Honduras & Guatemala.
This is similar to the above species but with larger, more showy flowers. It is a tender shrub to 3 x 3ft.(90 x 90cm) with hairy stems and broadly ovate to heart shaped leaves, covered in dense, short hairs above and tomentose beneath. The flowers are deep blue in whorls of 3-6 with a stickily, hairy calyx on short, lax racemes from July to October. The upper lip is hairy and the lower lip is marked white within.
Seed is occasionally produced, but propagation is by cuttings. Hardy to -3°C.

Salvia longispicata *Mart. & Gal.* 1844

Native to Mexico.
This species is a tender, bushy shrub to 4 x 4ft.(120 x 120cm) and similar to the previous two species but with many smaller, pale blue flowers in long spikes from July to November or even later if mild. The upper lip is white, dotted with short, blue hairs and the lower lip is pale blue and flared horizontal.

Seed is occasionally produced but propagation is usually by cuttings. Hardy to -3°C.

Salvia farinacea *Benth.*   1833
Mealy Sage

Native to Mexico, Texas, & New Mexico.
This is a half - hardy perennial to 2ft.(60cm), often grown as an annual and when grown from seed in early spring it will be in flower by mid summer. The leaves are thin and glabrous, ovate to linear with slightly serrated margins. The flower spikes are short and dense with whorls of 10-16 small lilac/blue flowers from June to October.

The form most commonly seen is **S. farinacea 'Victoria'** with flowers of a deep, indigo blue with purple calyces and there is also a white form.
It is often used in summer bedding schemes as it is particularly effective when mass planted.
It can also be propagated by cuttings. Hardy to -4°C.

Salvia 'Indigo Spires'

This is an hybrid of S. farinacea and S. longispicata raised at Huntingdon Botanic Garden in California in 1979. It is a tender perennial with a lax habit to 5ft.(150cm).
It is one of the most attractive, colourful salvias and very attractive to bees. The leaves are similar to S. farinacea but larger, being pale green, undulate and almost glabrous with serrate margins. The small, deep indigo blue flowers are in whorls of up to 24, close together on the long spikes to 18in.(45cm) from July to November or even later if mild. The calyx and flowering stems are covered in short, dense, purple hairs giving a striking effect. Hardy to -4°C.

Salvia cacaliaefolia *Benth.* 1848
Cacalia Sage

Native to Southern Mexico, Guatemala & Honduras.
This is a tender perennial to 4ft.(120cm) with distinctive, triangular leaves with entire margins. The flowers are deep, royal blue in short, branched paniculate racemes with two flowers per whorl, from July to October. The corolla tube is inflated with a rounded, blunt upper lip and a horizontal, curved lower lip and exserted stamens. Propagation is by cuttings. Hardy to -3°C.

Salvia involucrata *Cav.* 1793

Native to Central Mexico.
This is a tender to half - hardy perennial to 5ft.(150cm), dying back in winter. The leaves are ovate to elliptic, almost glabrous above and purplish beneath with minutely serrated margins. It does well in partial shade and will survive to -6°C when established. The flowers are large, deep, bright pink in whorls of 3-6 in unbranched racemes from July to  November. The corolla tube is long and inflated with short lips, the upper being covered in short, dense, pink hairs. The flowers are surrounded by pale green, pink tinged bracts which unfurl to let the buds open. A whorl of bracts surrounding the buds is known as an involucre, hence the name involucrata. This is a very distinct and popular species which is often known as S. involucrata 'Hadspen', but the form more commonly seen is -

S. involucrata 'Bethellii' which has a large, terminal bud which sits on top of the congested inflorescence spike and never seems to open. The bracts are deep pink, more rounded and the flowers are a slightly lighter pink than the species.

Propagation in both cases is by cuttings.

Salvia confertiflora *Pohl.* 1830

Native to Brazil.
This a tender perennial to 4ft.(120cm) tall. It is only hardy to about -2°C. The leaves are ovate with crenate margins, slightly pubescent above and covered in tawny tomentum beneath. The flowers are in whorls of 6-15 closely packed together (hence confertiflora meaning with crowded flowers), on the unbranched stems. The flowers themselves are not large, but because of the unusual combination of colours, are very striking. The calyx is covered in dense, brown hairs, whilst the flowers are short and blunt and covered in orange hairs. It never sets seed in this country. Propagation is by cuttings.

Salvia atrocyanea *Epling* 1936

Native to Bolivia.
This is a tender to half - hardy perennial to 6ft.(180cm) tall. It is sometimes hardy to -6°C. The leaves are ovate with regularly toothed margins. The flowers are deep blue with a hairy upper lip and exserted stamens. The whorls of approx. 8 flowers are closely packed along the flowering stems which often droop under the weight of the flowers. The most distinctive feature of this species is the persistent, large, bluish bracts and large calyces which together almost enclose the flowers. It is a very unusual and striking plant.

It does not set seed, propagation is by cuttings.

Salvia miniata *Fernald* 1900

Native to Guatemala, Belize and Chiapas in Mexico.

This is a tender perennial to 4ft.(120cm), best in a position with a little shade. The stems are glabrous and purple at the nodes. The ovate to lanceolate leaves are smooth and thin with serrate margins. They are pale green often tinged with purplish red in sun. The large, scarlet flowers with exserted stamens are in whorls of 1-3 and well spaced on unbranched stems from June to November. The corolla tube is hairy and the upper lip is hooded and hairy with the lower lip flared and blunt and held in an almost vertical position. The calyx is glabrous with deciduous, reddish brown bracts.

Propagation is by cuttings. Hardy to -3°C.

Salvia van houttii

Native to Brazil.

This is a tender, spreading perennial to 4 x 3ft.(120 x 90cm). It does well in a slightly shaded position. The leaves are ovate, thin and glabrous and pointed at the tip with regularly serrate margins. The deep, wine red bracts enfold the flower buds and fall as they open to reveal large calyces of the same colour and rose pink flowers, an unusual colour combination and very striking. The corolla tube is long and narrow with a straight upper lip both covered in short, dense hairs and a short lower lip which is the same wine red as the calyx, with a cup shaped central lobe. The flowers are from September onwards to the frosts and well worth waiting for.

Propagation is by cuttings. Hardy to -3°C.

Salvia madrensis *Seem.* 1856

Native to Western Mexico.

This is a late flowering, vigorous, tender perennial to 6ft.(180cm) with erect, stout stems, yellowish green and deeply ribbed to 1 inch across. The large, deep green leaves are ovate and roughly hairy with notched margins. The yellow flowers are in whorls of 10-12 on branched inflorescences from October onwards with the calyx and stems of the inflorescence being the same colour yellow as the flowers. Hardy to -3°C.

Propagation is by cuttings.

Salvia uliginosa *Benth.* 1833

Native to Brazil, Argentina & Uruguay.

In its natural habitat, this species frequents swampy places, as its name implies. In our climate, it is one of the most hardy South American Salvias, hardy to -10°C, maybe more with a protective mulch, as long as it is not too wet in the winter. It grows to 5 x 3ft.(150 x 90cm) and spreads by means of underground stems, which means that as well as being propagated by cuttings and division, offshoots with roots can be dug up. The small leaves are ovate to lanceolate, slightly pubescent with serrate margins towards the tips. The flowers are sky blue in short, dense spikes with whorls of 6-20 from July to November. The corolla tube is almost white with a small, pale blue upper lip and a larger, deeper blue lower lip which is horizontal and flared and marked white within.
It does not usually set seed in this country.

There are some species that never flower outside in our climate, except perhaps in a very sheltered position with little or no frost, usually by the coast.

These species come from the more tropical areas, where the hours of light and darkness are more equal than ours are in the summer. Due to the unaccustomed amount of daylight, they put on a large amount of vegetative growth which inhibits the flowering until the autumn, when the hours of daylight are more suited to their flowering period, but by then it is too cold and although they may sometimes form buds it is too cold for them to open even if they don't get frosted. They usually flower at some time during the winter or early spring given frost free conditions under glass.

Salvia purpurea *Cav.* 1793

Native to Central & Southern Mexico, Guatemala, Nicaragua & Honduras.

This is a tender perennial of vigorous, bushy growth to 6ft.(180cm) withstanding hardly any frost. Hardy to about -2°C. The leaves are ovate and almost glabrous with serrate margins.

The flowers are in whorls of 3-6 in short, densely crowded, almost continuous, paniculate racemes. The pinkish lilac flowers have exserted stamens and the upper lip is covered in dense hairs and the lower lip is narrow and horizontal. Under glass it flowers from December to March.

It does not set seed and propagation is by cuttings.

Salvia iodantha *Fernald* 1900

Native to Mexico.

This is a tender perennial, similar to the previous species, particularly in habit and leaf. The flowers are a deeper, more cerise pink, held erect in whorls of 12-18 from December to March under glass. They have a long, narrow corolla tube, a small, straight upper lip, both densely covered in cerise hairs and a vertical lower lip with exserted stamens and a small green calyx.

Salvia dorisiana *Standley* 1950

Native to Honduras.

This is a tender shrub to 4ft.(120cm). Hardy only to about -2°C. The leaves are large and pale green with a strong fruity scent. They are ovate with crenate margins and covered in soft, dense, white hairs on both surfaces, the same as the stems. The large, pink flowers are in whorls of 2-10 well spaced on unbranched, glandular, hairy stems from January to March under glass.

This is a nice plant for just the foliage alone, but it needs to be in a large container so the leaves are not restricted and can develop to their natural size. Also a lovely winter flowering plant for the conservatory. It does not set seed in this country. Propagation is by cuttings.